The Temptation of Silence

Literature adds to reality, it does not simply describe it. It enriches the necessary competencies that daily life requires and provides; and in this respect, it irrigates the deserts that our lives have already become. ~ **C.S. Lewis**

Also by Fabrice Poussin

In Absentia, (Silver Bow Publishing 2021)
If I Had a Gun, (Silver Bow Publishing 2022)
Half Past Life (Silver Bow Publishing 2023)

The Temptation of Silence

Fabrice Poussin

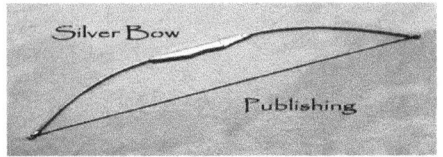

720 Sixth Street, Unit #5
New Westminster, BC
V3L 3C5
CANADA

Title: The Temptation of Silence
Author: Fabrice Poussin
Publisher: Silver Bow Publishing
Cover Art: "Earth – Day 1" painting by Candice James
Cover Layout and Design: Candice James

All rights reserved including the right to reproduce or translate this book or any portions thereof, in any form without the permission of the publisher. Except for the use of short passages for review purposes, no part of this book may be reproduced, in part or in whole, or transmitted in any form or by any means, either by means electronically or mechanically, including photocopying, recording, or any information or storage retrieval system without prior permission in writing from the publisher or a licence from the Canadian Copyright Collective Agency (Access Copyright).
© Silver Bow Publishing 2024

www.silverbowpublishing.com
info@silverbowpublishing.com
ISBN: 978-1-77403- 308-1 paperback
ISBN: 978-1-77403- 309-8 electronic book

Library and Archives Canada Cataloguing in Publication

Title: The temptation of silence / Fabrice Poussin.
Names: Poussin, Fabrice, author.
Identifiers: Canadiana (print) 20240370368 | Canadiana (ebook) 20240370376 | ISBN 9781774033081
   (softcover) | ISBN 9781774033098 (Kindle)
Subjects: LCGFT: Poetry.
Classification: LCC PS3616.O875 T46 2024 | DDC 811/.6—dc23

Dedication

To my steadiest source of inspiration,
the present.

The Temptation of Silence

Contents

Carnival 2020 / 9
Pépé Moustache / 10
The Simpleton / 11
Without a Chill / 12
23 / 13
If Ever I Were To … / 14
Bridge of Pearls / 16
A Life Pathetic / 17
In a Four-Wall Tomb / 18
Vandals / 19
Conspiracies / 21
Big Men and Little Ideas / 22
Hey Death / 23
Land of the Free / 24
Daydreaming / 25
Billboards for the Weary / 26
Portraits in a Door / 27
The World He Loved / 28
Joy of the Knife / 29
Take Time for a Slow Dance / 30
What Words He Chose / 31
Seeing Her Off / 32
Enter the Domain / 34
Coffee Shop Voices and Strange Accents / 35
Catching Fireflies / 36
Breakfast of Champions/ 37
Lasts / 38
13,8 Billion Years Ago / 39
Done With You / 40
Knocking At My Door / 41
When the Wrinkles Fade / 42
Law Breakers / 43
Out There / 44
Oils, Canvas, and Deeper Tones / 45
Landscapes for Posterity / 46
They Play the Piano with Their Souls / 47
Aches, Pains, and Broken Bones / 48
People of the Rock / 49

Trail Conversations / 50
When the Dream Gets Better / 51
Private Rollercoaster / 52
Beautiful Little Cells / 53
Friends in Heaven / 54
Beauty Masks / 55
The Temptations of Silence / 56
Her Image in the Glass / 57
2027 / 58
To Charles / 59
Good Son / 60
Tasting Time / 61
Asleep in the Cold / 62
Ancient Soldiers / 63
Poor Little Minute / 64
Bullies of Old / 65
Inconvenient Store / 66
Let Time Fly / 67
Discount Store Haven / 68
Crazy Thing / 69
Little Purses / 70
Dr. K's Tab / 71
Good Ole Jack / 72
Tic Toc Tik Tok / 73
Where Have All the Fishes Gone / 74
Landmarks / 75
Gladly / 77
Acid Campfire / 78
Games They Play . 79
Sunday Parking Lots / 80
Last Jog / 81

Author Profile / 82

Carnival 2020

Mardi-Gras in April
extending those days of glee
when revelers saunter the avenues
seeking another merry melody.

Yet they lack the luster of old
hiding in shame behind blue fabric
they wish they might breathe
inhale forgiveness in the shadows.

Stumbling in fear of the unseen
they stare at their kin on the other side
smiles erased by the feeble mesh
pleas fleeting within their breasts.

Pastels will quickly fade in the rain
sad reminders of brighter omens
ghosts soon to outnumber the crowds
amid clamors echoing into the void.

Pépé Moustache

I never knew the great man
who would have towered over the child
I was to be in the footsteps of
this silhouette of five feet and two inches.

Running before the war machines of Verdun
dodging steel, copper, and gas
he fell more than thirty years later
soaked with the liquor he never drank.

Quite late to make your acquaintance
I must have come crying
into the arms of a son who mourned you
for so many lonely years.

Your eyes so kind above a faint smile
did you know as you trimmed
the thick mustache that life
was to be so hard for your sweet soul?

You never knew me dear Pépé Moustache
yet I thank you for the son you made
the gentle gaze you gave him
a warmth only you could possess.

And so it goes through our generations
an old photograph barely faded
and perhaps you look down upon us
my father in your arms once again.

The Simpleton

Fourteen going on ten
dreaming in the third grade again
books in a hunting bag
only memory of a long-gone father.

Towering near the blackboard
staring at endless lines
problems for a young Einstein
he may cry if only he knew how.

Too old for a friend
too young for loneliness
trapped in a space without hope
dreams a secret to his kind.

He waltzed through the courtyard
attempting to keep a balance
in a town so small for his stature
racing home as he sped to the unknown.

Never to become an old man
seeking love in his despaired hours
he died on her doorstep
with his book bag and few memories.

Without a Chill

Another Monday
unnoticed in the early darkness
the echo of the familiar footsteps
has faded.

The air will remain still
where it twirled only a day before.

Lights of fire will lift
upon the cross
laid against the great hill
of eternal sorrow.

Slowly business will resume
suits and casual garments will hurry
holding purse, notes and Stanley cup
to reclaim their favorite seat

Door will open
early greetings with awkward smiles
as the sounds of keys permeate everything
and a semblance of life begins again.

Hugging a favorite drink
focused on a busy schedule
she too will enter the realm
as if nothing had changed.

Clamors will arise from exhausted voices
fearing the hardship in sight
none will notice that
one door is still closed
before the quietness of the tomb.

There was no warning
simply the unexpected
and perhaps a little speculation
and then nothing.

23

My tombstone will only bear a number
questioned by the passers-by;
born in the 20th died in the mid 21st
age 23.

Graced by a life of chaos and peace
I realized so little I knew in delight
and I could learn endlessly that
math may not rule my days.

Those who look at me will frown
at what they consider poor humor
and I will spread my sorrow for them
at the foot of the infinite.

Of course, I own the grey as well
as the grooves imposed by decades
yet I saunter amongst the giants of the forest
a child still.

Mature kin may grin at my antics
so unreasonable I will appear
I will continue on my path, a stumble here
a fall there.

Not certain that I will ever die
this heart will have no regrets unless
perhaps it is that I could have
loved you sooner.

If Ever I Were To...

If ever I were to jump off a bridge
I would pick the highest on earth
so I may ponder this decision
an index finger onto my chin
recall the good times, and foresee a smile
then, of course, I will pull on the ring
and open the parachute I never leave home without.

If ever I were to put a revolver to my temple
I promise it would not be to play Russian roulette
for I would load each chamber with a surprise
and certainly no gunpowder
since I might become death
hearing the scream of the silly cartridge
as it fell to the floor in its lonely agony.

If I did think of slashing my wrists
I would pick a clean blade dull as my latest joke
observe the way it reflected the blue of my ceiling
pretend that I were DeNiro and his 357 Magnum
but you see, I am no kamikaze and Seppuku
Is not for me since all I like to slice is
a juicy Georgia peach.

I might also think of getting a noose
like those used in the old West
but that sounds like too much trouble in this age
building a scaffold, stairs, and then hire
the hooded executioner whose mama
thinks he is an executive at Google
and brings home Christmas bonuses on the 14th of July.

I might consider the guillotine
and then of course, there is the expense
the cost of engineers, wood, and precious metal;
would it really be worthwhile for one big party
with only one guest in a white shroud
and a remote control powered by 4 double AAs
when I always buy triple AAs instead.

The Temptation of Silence

I realize there is too much trouble
in considering the dark things I could put in a box
and instead, go for my usual walk to the next town
carelessly frolicking with deer and squirrels
fall in the grass as I read another novel and just laugh
that I can still breathe the same air you do
and contemplate the next time I will hug you so very tightly.

Bridge of Pearls

I have lived on an island of rock, sand, and luscious trees
envied by the many who never find such solace
from the distance they know by the warmth of the hearth.

They might venture for a brief visit to my realm
as they keep their eye on the precious clock
they never leave behind for fear of a missed moment.

If only they knew that I too seek an escapade
a bridge of wood to the multitude they know
for the embrace of the one they ignore.

A mere instant in their world so I may collect the
stones of marble to prepare the way
for my many incursions under their heavens.

While they fancy hours of solitude
privilege to those who live in daily chaos
what do they really know of my paradise?

I cherish the day when at last I will find the tools
to build an eternal pass made of steel and glass
sheltered from the elements, safe from the unknown.

Better yet, I imagine gold and precious stones
paving the way to the beloved gate
where I have so longed to find my refuge.

A Life Pathetic

Half a century to no avail
inside the bustle of his world
he might be a phantom.

Did they know when he came
to life that little would change
as he occupied more space each day.

There was hope in their dreams
for a life well drawn onto the canvas
filled with a hundred and one clichés.

Who does not wish a throne of gold
diamond tiaras and sports cars
for their dear little offspring!

Fifty years drowned in the deep mirror
to watch harsher grooves on the leather
skin touched only by the sun.

Too late for everything he might stop
inhaling surroundings that wonder
whence this black hole came.

Tomorrow he will die unknown
of the only one he ever loved
a carcass atop a saturated landfill.

In a Four-Wall Tomb

She has walked to the end of the earth as they say
alone under the heavy rains of March.

When she trod on the path to nowhere
she could only think of the price of loneliness
shying from the very shadows heading her way.

Her gentle gaze of deep blue filled with the weight
of her unanswered prayer
lead tears gray as the threatening horizons.

She continued on under a force she could not see
pushed forward to lives she could not fathom
voids she had seen many times before.

Always the same feeling surrounded her
bringing her most certain surrender
among the multitude, utmost solitude.

Everywhere her thoughts settled for a moment
she only found the crushing of the abyss
fearing even the tomb she would find at home.

Vandals

In the glorious landscapes of red rock
they hope for the memorable hikes
through stone, sand, and mysterious silhouettes.

A little ride to the head of fantastic trails
a few bottles of precious H2O, a few snacks
and a song in your heart.

It takes so little to walk this joyful earth
since it is said it belongs to all
young, old, small, big, or even a little silly.

So why do we find so many scars
on queries of simple pleasures
in a realm that belongs to no one.

But they have done so, planting signs galore
the temporary billionaires in transit
for it would be a crime for you and me to spoil their gravel.

Private property screams through the trees
be careful not to park here, there, or even a little further
since we own this and the vista belongs only to us.

Residents of decades shed a tear to the dream
of retiring years in peace away from the city
at the door of the new Starbucks and Whole Food Stores.

Now the plastic surgeons have taken their world
from Lalaland to this recently pristine nature
to make it into a Beverly Hills a few hundred miles away.

Hikers talk of a little house near town
where wine and good food still flow
to find hotels even give them surprised looks.

You will find no graffiti, nor forgotten trash on the streets
you may want to immortalize the scenes of asphalt

and enjoy what belongs to the universe through the citadels of immigrant billionaires.

Conspiracies

No such person exists in a world
of alternate realities and post-truth
or they are simply others.

I watch them at the diner sipping
on a third pitcher of mediocre brew
at the club drinking their thirty-year-old scotch.

Idiocy knows no class or education
oddly as they recite the lessons of their masters
and I hear of aliens invading our bloodstreams

chips implanted in our brains before we are born
lasers aimed at local businesses by the powerful
and the constant scrutiny that reaches into our wallets.

It is fortunate that they will never know
the lunacy of the ideas fed by their idols
for only they know right, and I have naught to fear

of reprisals unless of course, it is to underscore that
I am the brainwashed one, finishing my espresso
snob of the elite, mastermind of the meek.

Big Men and Little Ideas

You can see them coming in threes
like the judges of old in a high tribunal
inquisition of sorts to prey on the weak.

They might be undertakers with their somber gaze
bearers of scythes swiftly they proceed
to the unsuspecting masses in the village.

You have seen them from time to time yet
choose to forget the ominous arrival as
if ghastly figures meant for a hellish fire.

They carry the good book with a sly smile
seeking another victim among the innocent
all before their next meal of grub and bones.

They can never do wrong since it is written
in words only they can decipher in secret
from signs on a rock to letters in silicon.

We all know these monsters far too well
who blend in our everyday happenstances
grinning at the carnage they can always justify.

Big men at six feet above ground they condescend
as we look up with fear of another stolen meal
vultures without souls they echo as if from deepest abysses.

Congratulating themselves for deeds no one can see
they rejoin the darkness of their abodes where the rottenness
of their spirits oozes into the entrails of the earth.

Hey Death!

I heard through a grapevine
that mother went on her way
one cold January eve.

The pain seized as the blood ran
and she seemed to wink
at the unsuspecting medic.

I saw her husband follow
when he was ready in July
to make a deal with God.

They do not seem to mind today
although the earth may have forgotten them
the infinite still vibrates with their tremors.

How is it, I wonder, to know eternity
share with all those souls, lives they never knew
in languages they never learned.

Dear Death, someday we will become acquainted
and spend this long journey together
but is it so bad when it is eternal?

Land of the Free

Buried within the shroud of her black glory
she waltzed into the crowd wearing that kind gaze
light beneath the perfume of her feminine days
she seemed to float in a dreamy fortress.

Behind the curtains of her last performance
she hid tears only she understood
singing of the distress none suspected
drowning in the sharp liquid of ecstasy.

Fleeting hugs beside a strange showroom
and she disappeared in another life
to travel roads and skies in search of something
a mystery secret to her though always hers.

At last, she speaks in the voice she sought
a surprise to all those who knew her
but what can a heavy soul like hers
mean to the willingly deaf and blind stranger.

Free she is sure to change this world
her immense heart submitted to the pain
a book upon which history will be written
in words which will sound a little more like a symphony.

Daydreaming

Child of ten, lost in the images of her,
he could not keep from drifting
into a land of wonders and bright colors
as the teacher spoke of words and angles.

Teenager, he remembered her yet
in a classroom made of boys and grown men
discussing physics and electrical currents
he only had eyes for her undefinable form.

Seven years gone in the large amphitheater
crowded with hundreds of puzzled souls
why did they need to listen to this eminent mind?
but he looked only at her in the light summer dress.

Nothing seemed to change as the decades died
squinting through the crowds he always found her
the weight of life could never impede his desire
as she breathed with the softness of his cravings.

Today he revels in the dream surrounded by wrinkles
yet he will never slow his pace following her aura
perhaps he will find himself closer to a last breath
to no avail since his love has never faltered.

Billboards for the Weary

It is good to know that in some regions
you cannot miss the great opportunity
driving the interstate at ninety, you can still
buy yourself a decent funeral for $4,999.

Who would want to pay five-thousand
for a ticket to a show they cannot attend?

We have to be glad that we can find lawyers
who will serve us for free until they win
a lottery with their vivid imagination
and a lawsuit for a few bumps and bruises.

Distracted by their grandiose images
thirteen feet above the wide asphalt lanes.

A wondrous thing it is for our insurance men
who paint themselves in so many portraits
from gecko to caveman to lovely matron
so we may need no attorney or undertaker.

Constantly reminded that for a grand or two
we may leave all our worries home.

Gladly you may cross a state line for a great welcome
painted at the side of a skyscraper announcing
dispensaries for something they call green
grass to be smoked and comfort to be found.

Another leg on a great journey to the red land
all thoughts of those social concerns vanish
and I will nap under the pines
alone on the trails to eternal solace.

Portrait in a Door

Clusters of words swirl in the depth of a strange realm
images flash to make motion of what was once so still
stories emerge in chapters of sobs, grins, and laughter;
scatological conversations through a fertile desert.

The apparition endures less than a moment
a single frame of utter simplicity to be held in a safe
a soft breeze penetrates with the slow motion of the gate;
waves pass gently through the ebony sea.

An aura comes to be borne and stills the hour
which needs no more to hold with a meaning for millennia
impressionist with the glow of Degas' juvenile dancers
rich with life for eternity in most intense serenity.

The hand on the frame which soon will close
gliding as if to the fragile envelope of the infant
her face remains in a tilt as she dares a light smile
she seems to speak, but sounds are trapped in the canvas.

Deep blue crystals to a profound soul gape to her will
the pose becomes imprinted on the unseen frame
a memory laden with the ongoing present
she creates the impossible, never to perish again.

The World He Loved

Gardener near the sky
thick gloves of green latex
protect her writing hands.

The air seems a little thinner
above the sounds of sirens and taxicabs
forgetful of the digital duties ahead, she smiles.

Beneath the band-aids inside the sharp cuts
she rejoices with the thought of a coming feast
shared with the only guest ever to enter her kingdom.

Surprising micro planet atop a cathedral of steel and glass
she has been a stranger to the world below
content with her daily visitor.

Oasis born of dark sadness
refuge from fears she knows too well
this land her own, it might be a beloved child.

Yet alone she will remain
for it was the city truly that he loved
below her pedestal to Heaven.

Joy of the Knife

It was too late in a never-ending emptiness
when he seized a wondrous blade
to plunge deep into the hated entrails.

What choice did he have but to destroy
a thing not a soul seemed to believe worthy
of a glance or perhaps even a moment's praise.

He might see the life slowly flow to a torrent
weaving its jolly way to an unlikely future
reddish as rust in the century old dust.

When it became too hard to smile
answering the same question with a pretense
all is well in an abode where all is pain.

Everything near and far oppressing his hope
why might he continue on the terrifying path
where everything points to a well-known abyss.

Sleep comes slowly in the frigid home
hollow as it echoes of eternal absence
when dawn comes all will be forgotten
for he already never was.

Take Time for a Slow Dance

I see you stealing a moment in the crowd
seemingly impatient to enter the next moment
next door, on the next floor with the next person.

If only you took a little time to slow your waltz
the great summer dress will still draw Arabesques
in the air scented with your passionate aura.

I wonder if you are still able to feel your
surroundings as you speed to another appointment
leaving behind all that may want to stay near.

A whirlwind of tears must dry quickly
when the observer remains in puzzlement
chilled near the frigid void where you once stood.

Will you please slow your step in the show
that teases space yet creates no bond
give me a minute for our everlasting slow dance.

What Words He Chose

An old film, played at unruly speed,
scratches and spots raced upon the silver
images of a man who no longer changed;
a strange statue so still it seemed a death.

Yet the eyes still glimmered in the dark
reflection of distant lights so long extinct
there was life in the shell of a man
monochrome but for a flickering candle.

He stared at the night heavens
as he contemplated the sterile sheet
scribbled with languages so foreign
he understood little of his ancient thoughts.

Syllables of eternal fancies floated
within his wrinkled soul as they ventured
shamelessly onto the unwilling page
to whisper words across time and space.

Silent for the moment searching
all he needed was the energy of magic
to invent a single word so he may be known
if of but one soul yet unaware.

Seeing Her Off

Last steps to a daily ritual,
the apparition vanishes once more,
at the corner of a corridor so bright.

Another duty awakens quietly each eve,
a life of an entirely different glow shines,
alive, and removes her swiftly from sight.

Time to begin new games, wipe other tears,
a little younger, a little prettier than these.

A mind has traveled back to a space unnatural,
she is reborn to the planet of little aliens,
so charming, so pure when they smile.

Leaving steps behind to retrace next day,
she will not return, only the future matters.

Meals to be made, beds to be cooked, stories
to fabricate, and comfort to the architect;
she accelerates; her name is called from afar,
the hour has come to begin another decade.

Seeing her off is such a lovely event;
incognito she moves into another land
private, protected, she seems to feel no pain.

Dissipated as she goes every day
she becomes again on the other side
secrets surround her, she floats with ease.

Nothing simple about her magic
like Mary Poppins, mastering the immensity
walking on water, sliding down a banister
she works another hour; one is not sufficient.

Knowing all her powers, she will create this night again
and to see her off is such a lovely event, anticipating

The Temptation of Silence

when she will return, carried by the joy of being thinking of the lovely event her encounter is.

Enter the Domain

For all the mistakes I have made
and the many to come that will
make you laugh and wonder why
I am such a terrible typist.

For the many lines I have collected
upon my brow at the corner of
the smile I rarely seem to be able to
wipe off even when I stumble.

For the elegance I cannot find
among the many magicians
in the crowds of worthy pretendants
to the seat warm beside you.

For the hopelessness which my birth
deemed essential to gift me
with such awkward manners
when I may need your embrace.

It is not pretty I know but
there has been worse union
than that of a goddess with a dwarf
so I pray my knee to the diamond.

Join me before the years part us
so we may meet again for all times
and I will be deserving of your image
in the sky mine faded on firm ground.

Coffee Shop Voices and Strange Accents

The times, they are a changing as Dylan once said
and has been singing ad infinitum ever since.

What did he mean when he uttered these words
with the strange accents of the sixties
a decade of torment like no other, yet
like all the many before.

There ain't nothing we can do to stop the madness
or rivers of words flowing in symphonic scatology
like, why would we, like everything's alright ya know
even when I drag my syllables into a deathly screech.

It is the way of the day to embellish our tongues
with the first neologisms that come to mind
bellowing guttural sounds that belong in
the oblivion due our futile thoughts.

But it is so important to sound carefree just
as they did in the fifties and every decade before
whatever the cost and what memories may arise
I may recall platform shoes, bell bottoms, and dirty long locks.

It is good to grow out of the nonsense of the rebellious years
pick up a true sword to take deathly jabs at the ailments
that plague our years and at last act more human
like, ya know, whatever, but for real, just become true!

Catching Fireflies

I recall long-gone days when
armed with mere little hands
the girls of my world
chased fireflies with their palms
cupping the light to save their glow
for the mysteries of their slumber nights.

Too often it seems their energy died away
a few hours into their captivity
a rebellion perhaps against the giant
I was eight years into this world then
angered by the arrogance of these
creatures who could enlighten my thoughts.

Imagine the faint wattage of an insect
I needed to gather a far greater number
to make a colony for my own village
a power plant at my fingertips
but time was scarce between classes of grammar,
music, Spanish, and other such errors of youth.

Thus, what choice do feeble digits have
but to borrow a father's musket and load it
with thousands of pellets of birdshot
after all the tiny boogers flew as well
so excited and certain of success I,
king of my realm, took a confident aim.

My rosy ears echoed of loud thunder
as I fell back under the jolt of immense power
my eyes resting upon the twinkles of our galaxy
showered now by my murderous intent
infinitely precious little glimmers slaughtered
and I had no choice but to cry.

Breakfast of Champions

6 AM on a brisk Tuesday they drive
a quick shower makeup session at the wheel
almost missing the entrance to their daily
mecca, cornucopia of greasy delights.

I slow to a crawl on the corner of Broad Street
and seconds again before the Walgreens
not to speak of another, grits and bacon
joint, a short while to Lowe's.

The same ritual each day, week after
tiresome week hurried by unspoken
clocks, meetings and frozen schedules
soon forgotten in a two-line memo to no one.

They go by the thousands to these strange
drive-throughs to speak to a muffled microphone
answered by a voice from beyond, it appears,
invisible to their unknown life savers.

Armed with questionable answers to their prayers
dripping with days-old dressings
wilted Romaine soggy fries trapped
between two slices of tepid bread.

I might scream if they could hear and beg them,
beautiful boys and girls in their prime,
before it is too late for the grave
for them to bypass the arterial nightmare.

Pack an apple, orange juice, milk, and cereal
just like mom used to do; just a minute or two
to sit at home and take a deep breath before
the gentle aroma of better Java.

But like a snake a million miles they go
into the hellish den that will consume their bodies
with the stress of a moment lost
the fear of an angry boss three times their size.

Lasts

When I lay so exhausted
I will fight to keep those browns
open for another moment
I will wish for a final imprint
upon my soul to be that
of your smile.

As it begins tiresome to take
another breath in our room
I will make every effort to
discern the scent of decades
that fragrance you wore so well
on your breast.

While it will remain easy
to lend and ear and listen
when you recall our bravest moments
with those words you speak softly
of private sweetness also
with your voice.

I know you will share with me
the comforting tea of our evenings
when we sat before the hearth
a mixture of grape leaves and honey
it will be a great reward to drink
from your cup.

Perhaps what I will cherish for eternity
is the gentle hold of your palm just as it was
during the first days of our little heaven
walking the streets of the great cities
just do not yet let go
those fingers of my adored prison.

13.8 Billion Years Ago

The moment I was born
in the mind of a giant at
the onset of the universe
I recall

not a glimpse into the light
nor a sound of the cataclysm
or the colors of the flash
I perceived

a hint of tingling in that which
would ultimately become me
without shape in solid or fluid
something sought

a way to another form
13.8 billion years to the day
that I may write this testimony
to the hours

to come and run astray
to another time, another galaxy
yet to exist in the distance
a future

unknown, billions of years again
what will I be then
a whole world perhaps if only I could remember
this moment.

Done With You

In a haze of fire and brimstone, the monster rose
perched on feet clawed of razor-sharp horns
boasting the large abdomen of an insatiable maggot
it wanted to kill the meek to fill putrescent entrails.

Done with you, it screamed through a gigantic hole
dripping with a venomous bile manufactured in Hades
as it continued to gesticulate its puny tyrannosaurus arms
claiming a land belonging only to the eternal.

Its snout red with throbbing blueish veins
the skin sweated with rivers of rottenness
birthing warts and pustules boiling near explosion
the thing was relentless in its desperation.

It claimed superiority on all counts
demanded apologies from those it trampled
doubted the sincerity of the blood it shed from their terror
never satisfied even as it annihilated their just hopes.

This incubus has come in our land
to devour the souls of those who still dream
of leading the simple lives of lonely beggars
spectators of the atrocity of this decadence.

Done with you, it vociferated again
as they walked away ignoring this devil's threats
it is hard for the cruel heart to know that
its power does not exist against the gentle soul.

Knocking At My Door

When you come knocking at my door
I may not always be there
when you come knocking at my life
I may have stepped out for a moment.

When you reach palm up for a gift
as you merely seek to help me
when you change your pose in the light
forgive my ignorance of your language.

If you attempt to peer into my soul
as I look away without a hint
if you take another step closer to my shadow
forgive me if I feel the invader of your world.

The day you open your gates wide
you might see me bowing before you
for the scars of decades do not vanish so fast
and I will remain in disbelief of my fortune.

Please come back and knock again upon this door
too solid, made to survive many battles
for the warrior inside is weary and longs
to tear down the fortress he never meant to erect there.

When the Wrinkles Fade

Age is a funny thing
when you live together for a hundred years.

He looks to the outside
and sees marks of the years on their faces.

Recalling the decades
he still owns visions of what the world seemed like.

It appears easy when you are eighteen
to picture elders as if they were dust already.

Things change if time does not really fly
trees die, glaciers melt, and mountains too erode.

The universe bears the signs of time in its own way:
black holes, supernovas, and newborn worlds.

Sauntering at the pace of a young lad
he laughs at those who would rather sleep.

She follows him in the trace of many a day
ignored by those who look to another century to come.

Loving as he was five decades before he knew her
all he can see is the beautiful girl of eighteen again and ever.

Law Breakers

Bearded as the first Vikings on these shores
running, rushing boats into the ground
they seem focused on a purpose only they
can fathom somewhere in obscure distances.

No rule may stand in their way
since after all no one exists but them
as they break every law of the road
laughing with ferocious yellow teeth at the children.

Love killers they spit a gooey tar into a cup of Styrofoam
as artificial as the so-called heart, hidden
in a cage of rusty steel and putrescent flesh
they hate everyone in a sea of self-loathing.

Carrying the weight of decade-long indulgences
they appear as if ducks on land
proud of the greasy stains upon dead skin
a 38 balancing uncomfortably around vanishing waists.

Children once they played at smiling
gorging themselves in their kin's hate
for everything not entitled to their miserable greed
pleased with the monstrous ugliness in the glass.

Law breakers they wait, hyenas in the brush
near city avenues and crowded highways
to pounce and destroy the joy of the meek
so they may reign over a country of the collapsed gentle.

Out There

There is a world out there
beyond the dense line of trees
the thick green hues they make
a haven where all things exist.

It's a realm of gentle moss
quiet streams singing with the rocks
under a delicate light of fire
blues so clear few are aware.

Food is aplenty at the end of a cornucopia
fed by the great care of all creatures
within reach of those who still know
how to live in a fantasy stronger than the dream.

This is the place where I meet you each night
while others succumb to restless sleep
tossing and turning in an ocean of cold fever
unable to see the pain of their longings.

Under cover a natural alcove
we lie with no other implements than our touch
tightly embraced into a unique form
you and I merged for eternal hours.

Oils, Canvas, and Deeper Tones

How does she feel
in this two-dimensional
world?

It has been so long
since she began her work
at the wheel.

She has never been known
to turn a gleeful glance
to her audience.

She may be midwestern
German, Russian or perhaps
Welsh.

Committed to the eternal task
her heart beats to share the blood
with her creation.

She keeps her soul secure
made of a forgotten artist
safe in a world we will
never know.

Landscapes for Posterity

What will those scientists think
in a thousand years when they come to
the buried grounds of northern Texas.

They once found dinosaurs
arrowheads, sacred stones and
great artifacts in those lands.

The great sequoia and giant redwoods
today dwarfed by the unlikely metal
to save green earth with steel wings.

What will future archaeologists say
when they discover the ruins of
electric powerhouses and rusted cans?

What an odd, excavated land they will see
in the same delight that was once Darwin's
at the foot of ancient wind turbines.

They Play the Piano with Their Souls

They close their eyes upon the keys
fingers floating above the ivory notes.

Deep breaths into the brass of
an old saxophone forlorn in a garage.

Slender bodies undulate with the waves
of melodies ancient as the universe's first tremor.

The great lady sings an aria to the stars
never to faint across infinity.

A friend dressed in the shape of evening
smiles as electricity vibrates from her guitar.

I watch mesmerized by the passion
unifying her body in all its strains.

What a gift it is to unite to the hurt and delight
of those who speak through eternal voices.

Rodins, Rembrandts, Mozarts, Hemingways,
Eisensteins, rest in peace now to ever live.

I too, contemplate the common interpreter of their tongues
to let my heart cry, moved by their everlasting impressions.

Aches, Pains, and Broken Bones

You hurt in the frame of your decades
on your way to the emergency room
again, on a Saturday like no other.

Labor continues well beyond the hours when
thoughts must rest into the night
and you hemorrhage another day.

You are alive in the image of a muse
carrying with her the dullness of millions
crippled by destinies not yours.

I too feel the hurt as it grows through the oceans
storms in a flesh I barely own
yet I rejoice in the hours we still have.

People of the Rock

More than fifty years, they say
they have been sharing the same story
of love and dislike with this paradise
as more come in to bask in their private sun.

Somewhere well north of four scores
they persist with the same teenage ventures
resting on a rock the Inquisition would have delighted in
when their fires went out in wintry rains.

Sharing a makeshift breakfast of granola and
apple sauce in a bag, they giggle and
tell me stories of the old days
good, bad, and ugly, but they return.

Their names escape me, their memory does not
beautiful under concrete wrinkles
they have brought new lives to this land
shared with me an eternity in a glimpse.

Trail Conversations

"How you doin'? she asks
not waiting for the conformist answer
too busy taking a sip of her holy water
wrapped in plastic and early morning dew.

"Good mornin'!" they claim in bright accents
from North to South and other climes
boasting those ivory smiles
as if tomorrow would never come.

"Have a good day!," the gentleman softly speaks
in the path of a wife of fifty years
but she seems more interested in this lonely sight
as I snap another memorable landscape with a superzoom.

Voices echo as if words were spoken centuries before
in my head as they shake my achy muscles
ignorant of my inner thoughts, friends for a moment and
soon I ceased to exist for the chance encounters of these
elusive friends.

It is an odd realization, albeit for a mere second
to feel human in the midst of a universe
that does not care too much
whether they think you good or bad.

When the Dream Gets Better

The night seemed painted in black and white
and a few shades of gray.

As he walked in an eerie silence
the cobblestones echoed with his hesitant gait.

The air was made thick by a floating mist
heavy as the lead of cotton dreams.

An avenue narrowed into a path
through tallest memento to man's fetes.

The knowledge of what he was to find
now set forevermore.

So long he had nurtured a vision and a wish
it was time to enter the world made for him.

Not to be alone at last a trusting soul
waited behind those imposing gates.

Decades in the making a realm real
built with the gentle illusions of slumber.

Private Rollercoaster

Rolling and coasting they went
through desserts, oceans, mountains
meadows and glaciers onto this odd path.

Decades into the journey now
still facing what may come
hand in hand never to look behind.

She, still the little girl of seventeen
when first he caught a glimpse of those blues
and she responded with the coy smile of puerility.

They played those ageless games
just as today in what some call the silver years
careless of what they may think as they pass by.

He looks and sees the girl in the white dress
teasing the pulse of a man who may be seventy
but she too sees a teenager in tennis clothes.

Perhaps their perception is distorted by
years they never saw as they sped on,
to them it is but days in their common youth.

They continue on the rollercoaster of this existence
rolling and coasting along the bumpy road
living every shock with infinite delight.

Beautiful Little Cells

One at a time they are born
little cells made like
pieces of an organic puzzle.

I wish I could have been witness
to the first fragment of you
when your heart began to beat

In its glowing warm world
deep within the passion of
two souls in sincere harmony.

I can only imagine your tiny thoughts
when you moved in a thick plasma
food for the grand being you have become.

Yet I look into your eyes today
and I see in the shine of those orbs
the many sparks of your first energy.

The Temptation of Silence

Friends in Heaven

Who will your friends be in heaven
you who try to survive in the park
your belongings in a found leather carriage
hoping every day to find the rusty bench
under the oak that remembers antebellum days.

How will you get by with those who cared little
for your antics when you had a little too much
proper as they were during the suit-bearing hours
too eager themselves to walk the old haunts
in mahogany and thirty-year-old bottles?

A girl loved you once, now living with assistance
children visit her from time to time in the sterility
of a space made for those whose dreams are in the past
little ones follow them in fear of the deep wrinkles
the tubes and orange bottles near a strange green bed.

No one has seen your thoughts in so long behind the hair
uncut for those abandoned decades without aim
and you sit it seems absent behind the glare
the paper bag and a borrowed lunch in plastic wrap
the only treasure you savor in days of nothing.

Soon it will be your time to march onward
to cross that threshold so many times recounted
and you ponder what awaits you there
an old photograph in your hand, of a smiling gang
will they be there for you to feel home again?

Beauty Masks

Beloved child she stumbled on a limelight stage
wearing heels made for a mother
cheered on by strange adults with fancy cameras
she pursed lips in what she thought a smile.

Frail legs swayed with newly found pain
hoses, mascara, and other devices
prescribed by an ambitious manager
she is six, might as well be twenty.

She traveled many ages and numerous cities
on luxury transport and first line air
sniffing caviar, Havanas, and cocaine
forms preserved by chemicals and a little touch up.

She recalls those days when it felt so good
to show angular curves bathed in two pieces
of thousand-dollar fabrics per inch
before the party to celebrate her twenties.

A monument now she feels nothing
under the artificial layers tailored for a future
walking to cheer on her replacements
so artificial the mirror reflects a stranger.

It has been many visits to the cold rooms
under bright lights again and silent walls
as she tried to recover a youth not her own
and succeeded so, in looking like another's ghost.

The Temptation of Silence

Do they hear when you speak of kindness
as the storm rages even within their dwellings?

Do they listen when you remind them of the evil
which finds a home beneath the rotten smiles?

Do they see when the world spins to a frenzy
into a hurricane dust of their lives' debris?

Do they watch as the earth's bowels burn
the last drop of dew on the cremated oaks?

Does it matter to them when she cries
near the grave that houses all her dreams?

Why say a word, why show them the eternal film
of the sadness that brushes past them.

Perhaps she will choose to vanish with her words
charming as they are, murdered by their ignorance.

Her Image in the Glass

Revealed at last in the oblong mirror
the image of another comes to completion.

She moves in her grandiose gown of the night
floating as she has achieved her every whim.

The glass has two sides as another world
mimics her every twist as she swirls.

Her eyes close as she no longer needs the realm
her lips sealed in a smile fashioned for eternity.

Her arms embraced in those of an unseen other
she might be dancing a waltz to paradise.

The reflection of her vanishes now to conquer all
eager to become one and abandon the former shell.

It is finished in the submission of him
too forgotten on the tile of a past empire.

Life eternal in the unison of abandonment
without a word, a mere sigh then an absolute self is made.

2027

She had to think of a date
a future not so distant for her story
a few words yet without structure.

Straight lines upon yellowed-out sheets
what could she dream of so late in the day?
The night too dark for even a thought.

Curled up in the ova the body remembers
arms clenched upon a warm chest
her soul still smiles in utter aloneness.

She may hear the sounds of crushing bones
so, the ruby mass will flow free as death
like an ink she so much desires for the quill.

A whisper and a grin on the frail envelope
the world she yearns clearly awakens
as she falls endlessly into the deep pit.

It was to be 2027 at the head of the new chapter.
She wondered what mattered so much about those digits
still in the silence of words only she understood.

To Charles

Shadow of Parisian nights
you haunt the city of lights
with your images of the poor
the prostitutes and the dying.

Evocations of the sublime
in emanations of the putrescent
you took us on unexpected journeys in cities
devoured by the magnificent maggots.

Your gaze still pierces through
the many portraits left behind
from beyond the frigid residence
under the soil of Montparnasse.

The genius of your rhymes echoes
with the power of the eternal
in a language universal
crossing all that is relative.

Has your heart really ceased to sing
beneath the mysterious chest
you who speak to all through the ages
of the implacable loneliness of this earth.

Sad man gifted with the passion
of a nation I can only imagine
a glass of absinthe with you
in a remote corner of your favorite dive.

Good Son

Laying bricks with a laborious mind
staring at the glue through thick glass
he had never seen a book that could
place an X to prove his existence.

I would watch the humanoid approach on two wheels
a sputtering beat powering a feeble breast
in his wake quickly vanishing earthquakes.

The mouth made sounds of an illiterate dialect
for a child to understand an awesome fete
he uttered vowels about a mother in passing.

I wondered whether it was truly human
behind the thick circles upon a soul
as it continued on an unimaginable tirade.

Upon another dawn he had disappeared
swallowed by a cloud of flames
somewhere at a crossroads to our wall.

The citadel continued on
witness to the monument I still ponder why
this son claimed his mother was likely soon to croak.

Tasting Time

The waiter came by to grab an order of ice and cream
in tones of soft flashy reds and nuggets of cocoa and nut
he attempted a snippet at the girl buried in the in-folio
to receive but a hesitant acknowledgement of his mere life.

Walking the steps of stone and cement gray as the grave
under a boiling sky, she advances against a heavy crowd
seen, she gazes at naught, fearing the instant of a contact,
the flesh shivers with the dolor of gates left a-gaping before.

In the dark room where the pen barely ceases for slumber
she keeps her eyes to the ink as it flows freely, endlessly
risking a brief distraction to the outside, quickly again
it is in her selfish privacy that she burns with life.

Only the home of solid walls of another time in history
provides the safety for a soul weakened among strangers
there, danger is set aside in unconditional reward
with the kin she made, the nest remains safe in the heights.

Like a flash she vanishes behind the drapes of another land
bars on the windows of her days unbreakable
she will once again unlock the chains of her domain
expose every cell to a slower pace, a taste of the instant!

Asleep in the Cold

I imagine your delicate knees under
the gentleness of eternal snows.

Your hands wrapped around weary ankles
head softly resting on the icy white pillow.

Asleep it seems, eyes closed in a dream
warm lips persist in the unlikely smile.

Ocean waters tease toes of a kindest step
pale with the assurance of safe existence.

Waves of dark and silk resist the storms
a shroud, they offer a shield to all dangers.

Snows continue their slow encounters
as many souls from Heaven to meet with yours.

Living one under the statue of a silky membrane
worlds breathe of passion within as you sleep.

No need to awaken your slumber; an impression
inside you holds the secret of the creation.

Ancient Scholars

Dust plays tricks on their weary gazes
alone in the ivory towers of their genius
the world may run topsy turvy around their homes
unaffected they seem frozen in the cradle of oldest dreams.

Lost in the midst of a cloud of stale smoke
pipes lay cold atop the pages of an antique
volume holding secrets of universes far away
in strange arabesques and magic formulas.

They may still smoke from time to time
holding the rare cigarettes allowed by an old friend
their hair grey for a little while longer
floats above the vivid thoughts of their youths

Drinks have dried in the hazy glass
cubes of ice wait for a spiritual marriage
as the light of those electric candles dim
on a world few still share with these relics.

Perhaps a last cigar will brighten the final years
spent in secret within the oaken walls
of a fortress built with decades of joy
in a thousand-year-old castle made for giants.

Those beautiful minds buried beneath the silver, the white
and the bold seem meek to the masses who have merely
begun, still they hold the wealth of all generations
as they quietly conceive miracles for endless futures.

Poor Little Minute

It died without another thought
from the one who lost her
uncaring in the middle of the street.

An envious eye prisoner of the curb
looks, as a vulture might, to seize
the moment no one seems to want.

Why do the lucky ones not mind
leaving such wealth behind
as the young perish in the fields.

It might be no more than a minute
yet I think of the dying mother
holding the hands of the beloved, tight.

She might smile for a little while longer
while her audience cries with joy
as they know she is finally at peace.

I too might pray for such precious seconds
to contemplate faint stars,
inhale a fleeting song of the wind.

It is like the dinner I did not finish
a table with a few scraps of birthday cake
memories to be held dearest.

This poor little shadow of a life
a ladybug in the hurricane
so brief it may be a treasure yet.

Bullies of Old

Their voices resonate yet in the distant air
oversized as their forebears had been
undoubtedly set for another day of torment.

Miniskirts to assert power over the less generously
endowed with olive skin and gentle curves
they need not bother to hide their mockery.

A push passing along the luminous halls of
plastic, lockers orange as infamous jumpsuits
to let the geek whimper behind a padded lock.

A word ornate with numerous daggers
thrown amidst the encouragements of many cheers
boyishly she contemplates the chained exits.

It has been a decade or two and childish games
have been forgotten across the oceans
if the cruelty still stings but a little.

They may meet again under obsolete lights
surrounded by tunes their children loathe
who then will brandish the Pennants of glory?

Inconvenient Store

Picture perfect copy of the crumbling shop
next door one thousand miles away
atop the grey peaks forgotten of civilization
it may be a living memento of canvas and paint
forgotten beneath the ruins of a shack
home of the artist decayed into oblivion.

The occasional semi shakes the remaining walls
as it speeds to conquer the mountain
but the locals continue on their numbing trail
not in a rush to reach a destination
unaware that they did once have a goal
their journey ended here on the oily concrete.

We pass another such relic of forgotten times
two old pumps with rickety numbers rolling by
the familiar fragrance of gasoline permeates the air
figures in greasy overalls throw unhappy glances at us
the enemy unwilling to stop and listen to a story
they go back to their spitting cans and liquid fire.

The scenery does not change much in a neighboring town
across state lines into an immensity of desert fields
half rotten wooden signs with washed out images
show a pin up girl claiming the prowess of a super fuel
only seventy-five miles away if you can make it
a joke well played on the unprepared explorer.

Faint neon in blue and white and in red claim to be best
during decades already dissolved into another century
fixtures of these unlikely landscapes the same characters
stand one foot upon the atrophied structures smoking away
the dreams they never had; they do not see us
as we slow for directions, fixed in their cardboard reality.

Let Time Fly

Staring at the large hands high upon the wall
they scribble words with their worn-out pencils
chewed to the lead by anxious lips
why won't the clock speed its course to recess?!

It may be that time has slowed to tease those who rush
for you see, none can wait to build that house
and watch from a safe distance the faithful buddy
who protects the roaring decades ahead.

From time to time some rest in the evening breeze
a week stolen from the busy streets made of gold
to drown into a sunset beyond the ocean line
the taste of salt barely seeping through their weary suits.

When wrinkles settle in the grooves of an aging tale
they may not run the race of their wasted youths
yet they still seem to set aims to an impossible future
raggedy limbs trembling to the threat of unlikely dreams.

It is the wish no one will be denied, as they stumble
eager to find a place in a history too large for them
looking back to years which flashed to crumbling memories
reticent as they may be, they must so soon bid their farewells.

Discount Store Haven

This one boasts an arm in a mud-soaked cast
it seems with many messages in gruesome sharpie.

Another laden with a makeshift tablet of cardboard
wrote a few words to retell of eternal miseries.

All have myriad stories to recount for the willing listener
a war gone wrong on the home front; many jobs lost.

Addictions to numb the senses of the old carcass
riddled by the traces of needles and unfortunate encounters.

Sitting by the entrance of the giant discount store
seeking assistance from those who shop for a dollar.

I wonder why they choose such cathedrals of sadness
to receive sympathy from hard-working janitors.

A stolen shopping cart nearby or a rusty bicycle
they might consider the outskirts of a country club

or the great malls filled with luxurious outlets
theaters, eateries, and overpriced brand-name shops.

Crazy Thing

Black or blue upon unknown smiles
decades with open eyes I have seen
with old ears I have captured their sounds
those ghosts will haunt me to my last breath.

Angry with syllables they can barely utter
grimaces have scarred the faces of babes
once full of joy they played on my street
now I can only make up those cries of terror.

I wonder whether I will remember
the brothers who ran to the parks
celebrated summer and July 4th
anticipating the song of carols in winter.

A crazy thing it is to ponder the memories
we all take with us upon judgment day
I hope they will embrace the peace of heaven
those strangers I saw yet last eve under their disguises.

Little Purses

They walk down the hall little finger up
as if holding a precious earl grey
in the company of royalty.

But it is rigid purses they carry
rugged like accordion cases
treasures they can never abandon
even for a minute instant of depravity.

Head up to size a lowly world
five feet above a ground too low
for them to squat and kiss in due adoration.

What possessions they hold in the portable safes
that they never part with the pinkish leatherette
and rhinestone incrusted even in their delicate palms.

Proudly they ignore the multitudes
wallowing in such grim poverty
insignificant as they suffer with fierce labor
while they do nothing but laugh at their stench.

Pocketbooks at the size of their true heart
they lack the wholesome vision of this lonely planet
hugging the power of a few fake gold nuggets
their poverty so much worse than that of the populace.

Frozen smiles tight upon their thin lips
like gleeful cadavers they walk in
in colorful disguises to hide their darkness
yet soon enough they too will be forgotten.

Dr. K's Tab

Portly, he ambled in his late thirties
gifted with immense knowledge of
a sixteenth century thinker
and a premature bald spot.

He knew the lay of the land
riding the rail every day from the city
too tired to walk another step or
perhaps his way with soft skills,

he relied on us his faithful pupils
fetch him a daily Tab and a dozen
chocolate chip cookies
he barely touched.

Preamble to the lecture we anticipated
now ready to belabor Medga Quinn
and her mysterious friends
as he busied his feet below the desk.

A wondrous distraction we expected
between a famous quote and
his memorable interpretation
his socks slowly coming off.

I never saw him slipping them on again
perhaps barefoot he scaled back to
his Greenwich village apartment
the brilliant mind now almost a Nobel.

Good Ole Jack

He knew Stanley in his high school days
so he did and that made him a king.

But while Stanley made movies not too far
from Simon and Art, what did jack do?

Jack read books so he could master
the romantics and their thoughts.

So he shared what he had learned
his hand upon mine as if I asked.

Old man with the moustache
thin à la Birds of a Feather.

Whatever are you up to ole Jack
Stanley's gone and so are you, I think.

All I can recall is that word on page 500
of the unending Emile, and your sweaty palm.

Tic Toc Tik Tok

They live at the altar of their newest derision
rushing to the smart device and a spot in the sun
enthralled by their own image in cyberspace
centers of the only universe they care to know.

They live, you see, an incredible life
in the absence of thought or reflection
posing as if statues of the classics
Mona Lisas of a long gone renaissance.

Soon their charade will adorn the fragile walls
of binary fragments long enough until another
surges with a lower cut top and more for all to see
moving pathetic steps as if a grandiose dance.

Long ago spirits vanished leaving souls devoid of humanity
now they roam the membranes of a strange galaxy
unable to find anchor in even the shallowest of grooves
upon lines of a story written on virtual parchment.

Time clicks away at a faster pace
out of reach of these odd creatures
who know nothing of human existence
and seek fame in five seconds of an awkward dance.

Many like them know an existence of make believe
empty shells in the flesh of little starlets
they smile and scream to be the ones everyone sees
only to return to the dust that never rose above the sewers.

The Temptation of Silence

Where Have all the Fishes Gone?

Sitting atop the cliff overlooking
the ocean vast
we hold one another
in awe of its innumerable mysteries.

The sun sets calmly for us
rises with deft determination
on the other side
of a blue horizon.

Not a sound
emerges from the deep waters
clean of all lives that once were,
ancestors some say to our kin.

Where have they all gone
why extinct so soon into fossils
imprints per chance left in the stone
that tell of so distant an evolution.

Landmarks

Five years old; she giggles
in flowery tights for winter nights
groggy for this early morning
tearing at the handsome wraps.

She might be boy; she is girl and does not care.

Five years have died since that Christmas morn'
a little more serious she opens presents
smiles and hands out hugs for free
in her woolen dress of green and red.

The family revels in the common joy

Fifteen comes about to find her in sadness
the world has changed without warning
she no longer wears those girly leggings
too careful with mascaras and eye liners.

Mother and spouse ponder her troubles

The day came too quickly for all
to see her pack suitcases in the old Buick
and move again to the old dorm room
where boys wait in line to spend a moment with her.

Alone in the dark she cries in confusion

She remembers her younger days
now mother to the face of sweet innocence
with no one to provide for her needs
glad that another holiday will be joyful.

In the mirror she watches her age settle

One day she will be there for this little lady
recalling what she felt when she knew so little
of a land so strange to her fragile eyes
ready to engulf her without pity.

The Temptation of Silence

And so it goes

Too soon she glances into the darkness
with no one to hold her hand in the sterile room
slowly she drifts into a warmer light
her wish perhaps, not to be wholly forgotten.

Gladly

Gladly I will take the knife
cut open this chest of useless treasures
beating hopelessly in an icy cage
and guide your hands within.

A final gift to you
to let you cup in your palms
the life which persists only for you
the closeness of your warmth to my death.

I will let you extract it from its prison
so you may do with it as you wish
for it has been yours for so long
perhaps you will cradle its fading rhythm.

To sleep without the fear of a monster
hovering with the hissing voice of the asp
contemplating from above as you smile
in the knowledge that I truly care.

Acid Campfire

It might be Tuesday in the midst of June
a calendar droops from a rusty tack
confused in its crumbling sepia tones
they can't quite recall who placed it there
or when, yet they have a vague impression
of a silhouette similar to theirs, decades before.

Someone set fire to a desk in the living room
to make a feast reminiscent of their teens
when they escaped to the dark forest
and sat around the makeshift hearth as magicians
when their dreams were still puerile
they could laugh without retribution.

It may have been twenty years ago or perhaps one
they have not ventured to the streets in ages
subdued by an existence without imagination
they slouch in boneless bodies
glassy eyes into landscapes no one else can perceive
they might well become part of the wooden floor.

They are five, perhaps twenty without a will
to stand or change the channels on the antique screen;
they did laundry once and left it to rot
it was weeks ago, should they ask the neighbors?
but swimming through inches of dirt
wallowing in remnants of forgotten orgies they lay.

Someday their abode will implode
for a mistake under the expected influence
all who have survived will finally find a brutal end
in the flames of oddly concocted hallucinations
for a life without debt in a pricey world
too weak to face the humility of decent days.

Games They Play

They rush to know the outcomes
glaring at neon lights in the arcade
their mecca as they invade the palace
filled with the latest fashion in
clothing, electronics, entertainment.

One silver coin is all it will cost to experience
an adventure with avatars in battles to the death
for one minute of adrenaline pumping heavy
in bodies made to last perhaps decades yet.

Maybe they will win big, beat all the evil ones
and play for another thirty seconds staring
at the running clock on the screen.

Tomorrow, in the classroom they will repeat,
with high anxiety, staring at the wall clock
wondering when they will be set free.

Racing home, they might avoid a family meal
stuff their faces with detestable substitutes for food
and cloister themselves within the shell of their den.

They only think of what will happen next
eager to know, excited to win, at any cost even when
this means life will continue on at the speed of light
little particles without true meaning.

Thirty seconds for a game, an hour for study
six to visit the grandparents, a month until summer
eighteen years before the children find a mate
and at last time to begin again under the grey
of existences they seem to have wanted completed all along.

Sunday Parking Lots

Clear past the moments of prayers and praise
they gather in pairs one to the west
the other to the east as if in a duet
tango of stolen moments of passion
they dare not leave the safety of
the warm SUVs by the end of a winter's day.

They seem to talk nursing homegrown tobacco
their eyes tell a different story
of lust, lies and a few hours in a motel
while there is a home not so far
where another waits fully trusting, watching,
with boy and girl, the weekly games.

How alone they must be these barbarians
idling their engines just hundreds of feet apart
they miss the old drive ins of their youth
when they would hide in the dark, share a soda
pretending to watch the gory double feature
holding each other tight, far away from home.

Soon the asphalt will grow cold again
to make room for another unlikely couple
seeking what cannot be found there
but the illusion of peace upon the black surface;
will they find their way to shelter again
or abandon their souls to this wasteland?

Last Jog

She smiled as she left
pro shoes adorning the svelte ankles
close-fitting uniform made
for the daily morning run.

The friend saw her off with plans
for a late lunch in their cozy home
when trees still shivered in the winter air
hot cocoa, the treats of gleeful youth.

See you in a bit, she said as she began her glide
into the fateful park, she knew well,
in the forest where life was trying to sing,
where she was known of all that lived there.

The police soon came when her pal called,
too quickly they found the girl
somewhere so bruised, so still;
foul play they said to the vanished soul.

She will not come home again
the cocoa has gone frigid as much as her world
all to a standstill for the fanciful runner
and a town that grieves with disbelief.

AUTHOR PROFILE

Fabrice Poussin is the advisor for *'The Chimes'* the Shorter University award-winning poetry and arts publication. His writing and photography have been published in print, including *Kestrel, Symposium, La Pensée Universelle, Paris,* and hundreds of other publications worldwide, and literary magazines in the United States and abroad.

Poussin is a professor of French and World Literature., Most recently, his collections *In Absentia, If I Had a Gun,* and *Half Past Life* were published in 2021, 2022, and 2023 by Silver Bow Publishing.

www.ingramcontent.com/pod-product-compliance
Lightning Source LLC
Chambersburg PA
CBHW052151070526
44585CB00017B/2068